I0407299

INTRODUCTION

Whether you are already are in the car business or are just beginning a Career in automotive sales, this book will teach you how to become a top producer in sales. Selling cars is a lot more complicated than one thinks, that is, if you want to make $100,000 plus each year.

There is no reason not to make a great income in auto sales just as long as you have a process and follow it religiously. This book will teach you the steps you need to take to achieve the sale. It will show you how to build a customer base that will bring you an endless income as long as you want. Like every profession, there are tricks to the trade so get ready to learn them. The rest is up to you. Will you simply read this book and toss it aside or will you read it often, making sure you follow the steps to success.

Do you already have a job selling cars at a dealership but are not making a six-figure income like you thought you would? Are you ready to hang it up? Well, get ready to change things around by changing the way you sell.

If you read this book and follow the process every day you will have the tools and knowledge to excel in the automotive sales business.

You must learn the two most important elements of success. They are:

1. Learn and use the Selling Process

2. Know your vehicle product

To learn the <u>process</u> always follow these steps:

1. Always build Value in you, your dealership and then the vehicle before trying to ever get a sale.

2. Follow the steps to the sale that you will learn in this book.

3. Know how to switch a customer from a vehicle you don't have in stock to one you do have in your inventory.

4. Learn the right way to do a "walk-around".

5. Learn what to do and what not to do on a Test-Drive.

6. Learn To overcome objections.

7. Get a Commitment from the customer

8. Close the Sale

9. Do a Professional Delivery including touring the dealership with the customer.

Become knowledgeable with your product. Your dealership should have all the brochures and training pamphlets you will need to learn the about the vehicles you offer for sale.

If you follow these steps you will become one of the top producers at your dealership and earn that six-figure income you have heard so much about.

Car salespeople that excel challenge themselves to learn about every make of automobile their dealership sells. They learn the unique features of each model and brand, and then seek out the customer to match with that vehicle. Everyone who walks into your dealership wants to buy a car. You've got to find a way to make them want to buy your car. You've got to find out what they need. People buy cars for a variety of reasons, and the automobile salesperson's job is to discover what those are. Successful salespeople are combinations of advisors and friends. The average automobile salesman sells between 120 and 180 cars per year. Top car sales professionals sell between 180 and 600 each year.

Most salespeople work on a commission basis, placing them under pressure to sell cars. Turnover is high because those who can't sell cars are quickly weeded out by the dealers. They are under pressure to sell cars themselves. So if you want to make it in the car business read this book and learn the steps necessary to make a sale.

Car sales require someone who thrives on the excitement of the deal and has a strong degree of self-confidence. Other important qualities are the ability to listen, a thorough knowledge of product line, and an understanding of financing options.

ISBN: 1-4116-5509-5

Copyright: © 2005

Automobile Sales Training and Tips From The Pros

By

Douglas Hensley

This book is dedicated to some of the top automobile sales managers and trainers that I have had the honor of working with and learning from. They are: Debbie R, Darryl Roberts, Ric Barker, Bill Lewin, Rich Ackman, Bill Roberts, Rich Paige, Bill Clutter, Mike Finley and Todd Hudak of Hudak Consulting. Through the years I have taken notes from each of these people and came up with what works so you too can earn a six-figure income selling cars.

(Don't just look for a job - build a sales career)

Are you considering whether to enter the automobile sales industry but are hesitating because you lack the experience necessary to make the transition.

If you have the drive and desire you can learn to sell cars very quickly.

To become a Professional salesperson you must be willing to make a commitment and train to sharpen your skills.

For you, as a salesperson, to excel you must invest your time to learn this profession. Simply calling yourself a car sales person and handing out business cards with your name on them doesn't make you a professional.

You must realize that you really are in a profession and you must learn it.

You must always focus on improving your skills and abilities.

Make sure you are spending time with the pros not the typical 7 car a month guy. Hang with the top sales people and learn from them.

(The basics of selling)

Qualify the prospect to find out who the actual buyer is. Make sure you're dealing with the person that will be making the decision to buy.

Learn your trade just like any other professional does. Read everything you can get your hands on to sharpen your selling skills.

Constantly ask questions when talking with a prospect. It will help you focus on their wants and needs. This will enable you to focus on the exact features and benefits your prospect is looking for.

You have to show the prospect that you truly care. They must believe that you, not like the typical salesperson, will do everything possible to fulfill their wants and needs. Without the prospect's trust all the figures, discounts, rebates and incentives in the world won't mean a thing to them.

Once you gain the prospect's trust you become a friend, someone they can trust, despite your competitors' lower price.

People justify everything logically when purchasing an automobile. This is a very emotional experience for them. This is exactly why you must help them buy an automobile from you and your dealership, not simply try to sell them a car.

Always reinforce the prospect's decision to buy an automobile from you with sound reasons for the purchase they are about to make.

Always send thank-you letters to every prospect you work with, sold and unsold.

When calling an unsold prospect always have a reason to call them back. Maybe you just got in a four-door vehicle that fits their wants and needs even though they wanted something different. This keeps the sales process flowing when you have a reason to call.

Your objective is to keep the buying cycle going – presenting alternative vehicles or financing, giving additional information or scheduling an appointment for the prospect to come in and test drive a vehicle. Once the buying cycle ends, it's unlikely you'll get a sale.

Always discuss benefits, not features. People care more about benefits than features. Learn that features and benefits are the same.

Let's say you have a prospect that has 5 kids and he or she is considering buying a minivan. Even though the side sliding passenger door is a feature couldn't that be deemed a benefit. Show the customer how much easier it will be to load the kids in and out of the van. Remind them how effortless it will be to load their groceries. Do you see what just happened? We turned a feature into a benefit. Now you think of more reasons why this one feature could be a benefit to many prospects with children.

(Learn to Sell value, not price.)

You will find that price concerns are usually low on the scale of importance to most prospects. So why is it the first question out of a car-shopper's mouth? Because they have been trained to ask that question. It has nothing to do with their wants and needs. By starting off a conversation about price it will usually prevent you from obtaining a sale. Always demonstrate the value of your vehicle before ever discussing price and watch your closing ratio soar.

Prospects make buying decisions based on:

- Their salesperson.
- The dealership.
- The vehicle and it's benefits to them.
- The selling price.
- The right time to buy.

Every prospect has motives when it comes to buying an automobile. They are:

• The affordability of the vehicle.
• The Convenience and comfort the vehicle offers.
• The security of knowing they are purchasing a safe and reliable vehicle.

- The pride of owning a new vehicle.
- The satisfaction they will feel when taking ownership.

(Doing The Basics Every Day)

You must do the basics day in and day out. If you want to make it in the car sales business. There are certain things you need to do daily to succeed. If you follow the instructions on the following pages you can expect to make an excellent income in car sales.

(SETTING GOALS LEADS TO SUCCESS)

Set goals before you begin work each day. Write down your goals including how many people you need to talk with to make one sale a day. If you have a 25% closing ratio with first time ups then you need to talk with 4 new prospects a day to sell one car.

Setting goals will help you rise above the other salespeople and will help you to determine your own success. If you fail to set goals you have no plan of action and will not be focused. If you are not focused you are already dead in the water. The same applies if you have no plan of action.

By setting daily goals you are setting up your plan of action for the entire week and month, which will lead to yearly goals. Goal setting will help you earn a six-figure income.

Keep your goals within reason, but always try to do 01% better than you did the day before.

(Lets look at a sample goal)

You set a goal to sell 20 cars this month.

You close 25% of your prospects each month.

You need 80 prospects to sell 20 cars.

So now you know how many people you must talk to each month in order to sell 20 cars.

(Know your Inventory)

Walk the lot daily checking out your dealership's inventory. Check out every new vehicle stocked in and placed up for sale. You need to know as much as possible about every vehicle on the lot. Learn the options, the features and benefits of every car, truck van and SUV on the lot.   Take notes if necessary and memorize the features of each vehicle so you are prepared to tell the prospect about the inventory.

(UNSOLD PROSPECTS)

Again, contact every unsold prospect you can. Find a reason to call them. Maybe you have found a similar vehicle they were looking for. Maybe you have found a vehicle that is comparable to the one they wanted at a reduced price.

Most people can be switched from what they want to what they need. Most prospects are impulse buyers. What they want and what they really need are usually two different things.

That's where you can take control of the buying cycle. Tell the prospect why they need a different vehicle. For example, if a mother of two comes into the dealership and wants a 2 door coupe she will hate the car once she begins battling trying to get the kids in and out of the back seat. Once she hates the car she will hate you so forget about her buying another vehicle from you or sending you referals.

A good salesperson would steer her to a four door vehicle for that reason alone.

Without finding a reason to stay in touch with your unsold customers it will cost you thousands of dollars a year. Call them every holiday, call them on their birthday and anniversary. Call them even if they bought a vehicle elsewhere. By staying in touch with every prospect you can this will earn you more referrals than you could ever imagine.

Spend a few years following these rules and you will have such a referral customer base that you probably won't need to ever take a fresh lot up. Take a look at the pros who never take a sales call or fresh lot up.

How do you think they got to this point in their career? From referrals. They built this referral base because they stayed in touch with their customers, sold and unsold.

(Why You Don't Want To Switch Jobs)

The only way you can build up the referral base that I just mentioned is to plant your feet at one dealership and pay your dues.

Once you are in this business you will be told by salespeople who leave your company how the grass is greener at another dealership. If you fall into that trap you will never build your clientel base. You will end up working at one dealership after another. The grass is as green as you make it so don't start switching jobs. You need to understand that when you enter automobile sales you have just begun working for yourself.

Why do I say that? Because the dealership pays for a building for you to work out of. They pay all utilities for that building. They pay for the advertising and then give you thousands of dollars worth of inventory to sell each month. Most even pay for your business cards.   All you have to do is find a buyer to sell the inventory to.

Whenever you are not face to face with a customer on the lot or are on the phone with a prospect wouldn't it be fair to say you are unemployed at that time? So do you see how important constant follow up is?   Again, You are in business for yourself. If you hang outside with the 7 car a month guys you will become part of that group. I cannot stress how important it is to constantly be on the phone calling everyone you can if you really want that six figure income.

(Learning To Fact-Find)

Learn to fact-find by asking open-ended questions.

Fact-finding questions enable you to gather the information you will need in order to fill your prospect's wants and needs.

Take the time to listen to what your prospect says.

Let's look at some examples of fact-finding questions:

- "Who else will be involved in picking out the car?"

- "How will you use the car?"

- "What type of vehicle are you driving now?"

Never ask a question and answer it yourself before the prospect speaks.

Here is a good example"

Salesperson: So how did you like the way the car drove? It handled great didn't it?

By making this mistake you have just taken away the opportunity for the prospect to tell you what they think.

Train yourself to pause after asking an open-ended question and wait for the prospect to respond.

(FOLLOWING UP SOLD PROSPECTS)

Call back sold customers twice on the first month they purchased a vehicle from you. Then call on a quarterly basis. Call them on their birthday, anniversary and every holiday. Always ask for referrals before you end the conversation. If you don't ask the person on the other end of the phone they won't volunteer the fact that they probably know someone in the market for a vehicle.

Again, while the rest of the sales people are huddled around in a crowd on the lot smoking cigarettes and shooting the bull you work the phone as much as possible. That's what will earn you $100,000 a year while the other sales people are earning $30,000.00

Here is a good script to use when you are preparing to end a phone conversation; "Mr. / Mrs. Customer before I let you go could I ask a small favor?" (PAUSE) "Here at 123 Motors we pride ourselves in the fact that we do most of our business from word of mouth,... from customers just like you who refer other people to shop us for their next vehicle. I was just wondering who you might know,... maybe not right now, but sometime in the near future, that might be looking for a vehicle?"

I promise you if you use this script every time you talk with someone on the phone it will help you sell an extra 3 or 4 cars a month. Do this with everyone, even the person calling in about an advertised car for themselves. Do not let anyone go until you ask that question.

(You Must Prospect Everyday)

One of the best places to prospect is in the service department waiting area. Ask the customer what they are having repaired. Find out the mileage on their current vehicle. Ask how much they are having to spend on that repair. You will find that a lot of people will trade their car right on the spot if you assure them that your dealership will take their car in trade and you can personally help them pick out a new one without having to pay for that expensive repair.

Hand out your business cards wherever you go. Do you stop every morning for a cup of coffee before arriving at the dealership? If so, introduce yourself to the clerks and get to know them. Let them know what you do. Ask them to pass out your cards to anyone they talk to that is in need of a new car. Convenient store clerks see almost every car that pulls on their lot so why not ask them to help you by telling people in old vehicles that you can help them get a new car. You might have to pay the store clerk a few bucks every time they get you a sale but I'm sure you would be happy to do so. Do you attend Church or belong to any organizations? If so, make sure everyone knows who you are and what you do.

(MEETING AND GREETING THE PROSPECT WITH THE PROPER APPROACH)

People buy from people they like so your goal is to make the prospect gain a positive image about you from the start.

Always:

- Always greet the prospect as quickly as possible.

- When speaking to them always call them by their name.

- Make sure they know your name.

- Sell yourself to the prospect.

- Sell your dealership by telling them about the company and what it has to offer besides the sale.

- Always ask open-ended questions while building rapport with the prospect.

- Be sincere.

- Remember to always ask open-ended questions using words like: when, who where, what and how.

(Sell the dealership before selling the Vehicle)

As I mentioned earlier your goal in the meet and greet is to establish rapport with the prospect, gather fact-finding information and then determine the prospect's wants and needs.

Did you know that most prospects make buying decisions in a precise order. The first buying decision they make is about you, the salesperson, and is always made during the meet and greet. If you fail to follow the process you can plan on watching your customer leave without buying.

The prospect's second buying decision is about your dealership and what it has to offer them. Every car dealership is basically the same to a car buyer. They all have a building and sell metal with four wheels. So what makes your dealership any different? If you can answer that question to your customer you are already on the road to the sale.

Find out if the customer has ever been to your dealership before. If so, make sure you find out how their visit went and be prepared to overcome any negative thoughts or comments the customer may already have.

Does you dealership have a rewards program? Do they offer discounts on repairs and parts after the sale? Whatever it is that sets your dealership above your competitors make sure you convey that information to your prospect. By doing this you are helping your prospect decide to do business with you and your dealership.

The way you meet and greet the customer is the most important step to a sale. You won't get to first base with any prospect if they dislike you from the start.

Let's forget about selling cars for a moment. Have you ever been to an electronic store and instantly did not like your salesperson? Did you distrust them from the beginning? Have you ever thought to yourself you wouldn't by anything from them?

Ask yourself why you felt that way. What made you dislike or distrust that particular salesperson? Were they too pushy? Were they sloppily dressed? What was it they made you form a negative opinion of them from the start? If you just thought about these questions then you have to see how important your first impression is?

Do you dress the way you would expect someone to if they were about to advise you on a major purchase of $25,000 or more?

Did you ever wonder what a customer thinks when they pull in to your dealership and see five or six salespeople standing outside the front of the building smoking and waiting for them like a pack of vultures? Has this ever happened to you? What kind of impression did you have?

Always separate yourself from the crowd so the customer does not view you in that same light.

When approaching the prospect always greet them with a sincere smile so they feel you are truly glad to meet them.

Tell the prospect your name, ask for theirs, pause and wait for them to respond.

Welcome the prospect just like you would your best friend or a long lost relative who just arrived at the front door of your home.

(Find Common Ground)

Learn to establish some common ground and find some common interests with the prospect. Set aside trying to sell a car for a few minutes and talk about the prospects wants and needs. Ask where the prospect lives and works. Maybe you will know someone that works with them or possibly someone who lives on their street. Maybe you sold a car to one of their neighbors? If so, you have already begun establishing some common ground. By following this simple rule you will make the prospect feel comfortable with you.

(Don't Invade The Prospect's Space)

Sales people have been taught to walk directly up to a prospect, give a firm handshake, exchange names, and welcome them to the dealership.

This, to me, can be a mistake if you invade the customer's personal space. Did you know that people have three general comfort zones, home, work, and their vehicle? Believe me when I say a car dealership is not considered a comfortable place to visit. Most people shopping for a car are very leery of car salespeople for many reasons. Some have had credit problems in the past and have already been turned down at the dealership up the road. Some have been high pressured at another dealership and some dread the thought of going into debt.

When a salesperson greets a customer aggressively or in any manner that sheds a bad light on them this will usually prevent a sale immediately. You will not get a second chance to make a good first impression. Make sure you follow the steps to the meet and greet but give the customer their space.

How To Handle The Dreaded

"I'M JUST LOOKING"

Never ask a prospect if you can help them when doing the MEET and GREET. By asking a customer if you can help them you are setting yourself up to be told they are just looking.

Since most salespeople have heard this phrase a million times ("I'm just looking) you must learn to beat them to the punch. After you do your proper meet and greet ask the prospect if they are out looking around?"

By doing this you have prevented the prospect from telling you they don't need any help and they want to look around by themselves. This also tells the customer it is okay to look around at your dealership and they don't have to feel pressured by doing so.

(Fact Finding and Transportation Needs Analysis)

Again, always determine the prospects' wants and needs before you steer them toward the inventory.   Ask questions to determine how they plan to use their new vehicle. Always ask questions about the customer's lifestyle. Find out about their job, family and hobbies. Ask who the lucky one is that will be getting a new automobile.

Most people buy similar type vehicles to the one they are currently driving so ask questions about their current vehicle.

Steer clear of asking the prospect about

their credit history while out on the lot. This will put them on their defense even if they have excellent credit.

A large majority of buyers will want to buy a new vehicle for around the same price as they bought their last one for. Most people have a shopping pattern. They usually buy the same way so it is important to ask questions that will give you that information.

By asking fact-finding questions it enables you to know if you are dealing with a customer who is upside down in their trade, or may have special finance needs. This information will help you obtain the sale.

Learn to ask the following type of fact-finding questions:

1. Where did you buy your current   vehicle?
2. Did you buy it new or used?
3. How long have you owned your current vehicle?
4. So, what brought you to our dealership?
5. Have you ever visited our dealership before?
6. Was there a particular reason you bought your current vehicle?
7. What is (or was) the monthly payment?
8. Are you looking for the same type of vehicle or something different?

Once you have asked these questions you should be armed with the information you need to steer the customer to vehicles that are within their wants, needs and financial goals.

TALKING PRICE ON THE LOT IS A (NO-NO)

If you talk price on the lot you can't build value in your vehicle. The lot is never the place to talk price.

Build value in your vehicle; get the prospect excited about it and then talk price. If you allow yourself to be like other salespeople and give the customer a price in the very beginning you will never be able to build value or create the excitement of owning that vehicle.

By not talking price on the lot it allows you to learn the prospects wants and needs so you know how to help them choose the right vehicle.

If you follow the sales process outlined in the earlier pages it will allow you to stay off price until you are ready to write up a proposal.

Customers have been trained to ask for the price of a vehicle early on but it is not the price they are buying. They are buying an automobile to fill their wants and needs. Keep them off of the price question by asking open ended and fact-finding questions. Don't worry about selling a vehicle based on the price, rebates and incentives until it's time to write up the deal on a car that fits the prospects wants and needs.

Always respond to price questions by promising to get the prospect
a price, then, continue on with the steps to the sale.

Tell the customer you will be happy to get them your dealership's best price on any vehicle. Explain to the prospect that you will go over all the taxes and everything else with them so they know exactly how much the vehicle will cost. Tell them before you do that you need to show them a few vehicles to make sure they land on the one that best fits their wants and needs.

Talking price on the lot will greatly lower your test-drive ratios. It is very difficult to regain control of the selling process after your prospect has been given a price. Attempting to build value after the prospect has been given a price is difficult because the prospect has already determined the value in his or her own mind.

If you give the prospect a price first you will find it more difficult to get them to test drive. The test drive allows you to turn features into benefits better than anything else. Test-driving a car builds mental ownership. Without mental ownership you will find it very difficult to close a deal.

Down payment, taxes, monthly payment and the trade in price of the prospect's vehicle can also mean price to a customer so try to stay clear of any figures until you are inside the dealership sitting down face to face with the prospect.

(WHAT TO DO WHEN THE PROSPECT SAYS HE GOT A PRICE DOWN THE STREET)

How will you handle it when the customer says they got a price from another dealership and your dealership need to beat it to earn their business. Traditionally sales people were trained to ask what price the competitor gave them. By doing so we force our customer to lie to us. The Prospect knows the price is $16,000, but they tell you, "$14,000 out the door."

Without the proper come back this creates problems for both you, the salesperson and the customer. First of all you know you can't sell your vehicle for $14,000. And the customer knows he can't buy the car for $14,000 down the street. So now the only way the prospect can save face is to beat you up on price. The final outcome after two or three hours of going back and forth from the prospect to the desk is usually the same. You are left with no deal or a mini deal, which all sales people hate.

So let's take a look at how we can overcome this:

CUSTOMER: I got a price down the street and you have to beat it to earn my business.

SALESPERSON: Thanks for sharing that with me, but I need you to do me a favor. Keep those figures in your head for now. It wouldn't be fair to you or my dealership to try and over come that at this stage. Please allow me to present my dealership's figures and then you can tell me what you think.

Now assure the prospect you are confident that once you have reviewed your dealership's figures with them that they will want to do business with you and your dealership. (Be confident when you state this)

Now is the time to give the prospect an out so he doesn't lose face by accepting an offer from your dealership higher than the one he told you he got down the street. Tell the prospect If they are not pleased with your figures you wouldn't expect them to buy. And then tell them if they are not pleased with your figures to please tell you so.

By following this approach you will find it actually shortens the sales process. Your customer will begin to like and trust you immediately because you're letting them know you do not expect any commitment from them unless they wish to make one. By following this process you have eliminated the same old gibberish they heard down the street and changed their perception of car salespeople. At least you have made them perceive you as honest and caring and not just someone who wants to make a dollar off of them.

You have to remember that you can't control the customer but you can only control the selling process. If you can understand the difference you'll find that you are actually serving your customer instead of giving your manager an excuse as to why they didn't buy from you.

(Transportation Needs and The Selection)

Always try to select vehicles that fulfill your prospects wants and needs. Never fail to do this even if the prospect already knows what vehicle they are interested in. By following this process it allows you the chance to offer lower priced vehicles that also meet the customer's wants and needs before showing them the vehicle they are interested in.

By offering lower priced vehicles from the onset it prevents the prospect from landing on too much vehicle for their budget. Allowing the prospect to pick out more car than they can afford without having some alternative vehicles picked out first will cause you difficulties when trying to switch them to another vehicle.

(DRESS THE PART)

Your appearance always makes the first impression on the prospect. Your dress is an important part of how a prospect will perceive you as a professional salesperson.

Most people shopping for automobiles have had prior negative experiences at car dealerships and their salespeople so look professional and act professional.

There is no second chance to make a great first impression.

Always remember to keep your clothing pressed and cleaned and always make sure you shine your shoes when needed.

(BUILDING VALUE IN THE SALES PROCESS)

One of your best closing tools is: Value!

Have you ever sold a vehicle to a customer who could have bought it for less at another store? You know you have. In fact, if a customer drove out of your dealership and went to another one down the street you know the other dealer would beat your price? So how did you get the prospect to buy from you? Simple. You built enough value for them to make the decision to go ahead and buy from you.

(The Payment Issue)

Here is an example how to stay off price early on in the selling stage.

Prospect: What will the payments be on this car?

Sales Rep: Good question. As soon as we go inside and sit down I'll get you all the terms, including price, down payment and monthly payment. But, Of course, this will depend on your choice of vehicles and equipment. Were you looking for a 2 door or 4 door car?

(The Trade-In Issue)

Here is an example of how to stay off the trade-In price early on in the selling process:

Customer: Can I use my trade-in as a down payment.

Sales Rep: I don't see any problem with doing that. After we make a deal my dealership will pay off your vehicle and apply any equity towards the down payment. Are you interested in a new or pre-owned vehicle?

As the sales process continues keep asking fact-finding questions.

(Understanding Women Buyers)

You, as a salesperson, need to understand that there are real differences between men and women when it comes to buying an automobile. Women do their homework online more then men. They usually spend several hours gathering information about vehicles before ever visiting a dealership.

Women buy 50 percent of all cars and light trucks sold, and they have a say in about 75 percent of all vehicle purchases.

You better learn to develop a relationship with every woman you talk if you want to make the sale. You must find out what her needs are. Ask her what she likes and dislikes about her current car and what she expects of her next automobile.

Never refer to a woman shopper by any slang name such Babe, Honey or Sweetie. This will lose you the sale 8 out of 10 times.

Never tell the woman shopper to bring her husband back with her at another time. This is an insult and a slap in the face to women buyers.

No woman I know ever goes car shopping just to have something to do. If you have a woman on your lot 8 out of 10 times she is a serious buyer so treat her as such.

When upping a couple on your lot give both the man and the woman your business card. This immediately tells the woman you consider her an important part of the buying process.

When you take the couple on a test drive, make sure she gets a chance to drive the vehicle.

Address half of all questions to the woman. If she asks a question answer her not the man with her.

When a woman comes in to shop around before bringing her husband to the dealership take the time to earn her business so she will return.

(TAKING THE PROSPECT FOR A TEST DRIVE)

After showing the prospect the features and benefits of the vehicle they have chosen it is time for the test-drive.

Pull the vehicle up to the front of the dealership. Make a big deal out of it. EXPLODE THE VEHICLE by opening everything. Turn on the Lights, open the trunk, hood and doors, tune the radio, adjust the temperature, and slide the seat back. Walk them around the car. Point out all the options, features and benefits.

Present the car with excitement. Excitement breeds excitement.

Never ask a prospect if they would like to go for a demo drive. Get the customer to climb in on the passenger side. If you ask the prospect to go on a demo ride you are asking for an excuse from them not to go right now. Car buyers look at taking a demo ride as a commitment to buy so don't ask, just take them on a test-drive.

Once you have the prospect sitting on the passenger side show them how things operate. Once you complete this step ask the buyer to close the door. Start the engine and drive to a safe spot where you will now have the prospect drive. Make sure you show them how everything works again before they drive the vehicle.

When you near the dealership on your return begin asking questions. Ask if they like the way the car rides and drives. Ask if the features and benefits that the vehicle offers are what the buyer had in mind.

Never ask the prospect to 'buy' while on the test drive.

As you arrive back at the dealership remember to ask about the alternative vehicles you presented earlier. This will tell you immediately if your prospect wants the particular automobile the just test-drove.

(BUILDING MENTAL OWNERSHIP)

As you have already learned prospects make buying decisions based upon you, the dealership, price and the benefits your vehicle has to offer them. Once you have led them to this point in the selling process they only have one decision left and that is when to buy.

You would be surprised at how many sales people drop the ball at this stage of the selling process. Now is the time to ask them to step inside and go over figures.

At this stage of the selling process if you asked every prospect to do this your success rate would rise dramatically. Don't be one of those sales professionals that never ask the customer to come inside and go over the numbers.

(The Fear of Committing, The Write Up and The Close)

Again, ask the prospect to follow you inside so you can go over the figures with them. If you sense any apprehension from the prospect make certain you assure them you do not expect them to buy the vehicle at this point, that you are just going to go over the figures with them. This usually makes the customer feel at ease so you have the chance to present the deal.

(ASK FOR THE SALE)

After you present the figures to the prospect now is the time to ask them to buy. If they say no or give you an excuse why they want to wait ask them what is preventing them from buying now. Once you find out what it is try to overcome that objection. If you can't do it on your own go get your closer or manager to see if they can help the prospect over come their fear of commital.

If the customer makes a counter offer on the vehicle explain again all of the features and benefits that your vehicle has to offer them and explain why your manager gave you those figures. Tell them about the selling price, tax and title fees, reconditioning fees, their trade in price and anything else that will help substantiate your dealer's selling price.

When going back and forth between the customer and your manager make as least amount of trips as possible. This always upsets the customer. Always remember to let the customer know you arew working for them as you do go back and forth.

(Closing means asking the prospect for an act of commitment)

Again, 60 percent of all salespeople never ask for the sale. Don't let yourself fall into that group.

Your first close should go something like this: "If we can (What you want to take place), can you think of any reason why we shouldn't (The desired act of commitment)?"

Immediately acknowledge any objections with one of the following statements: "I see," or "I understand,". Let the prospect know you can see why they might have some concerns and then get back to selling them the vehicle.

 You second close should go like this:

- Acknowledge the prospect's objection.

- Review and establish all areas of agreement between you and the prospect.

- Mention another feature or benefit the vehicle has to offer.

- Ask for the sale again.

Your goal is to uncover the real reason the customer is refusing to buy now. You will find that many times the customer will not tell you the real reason why they won't commit until you pin them down.

Your third close should go like this:

- Acknowledge any objections;
- Review and re-establish all areas of agreement between you and the customer;
- Uncover the customer's real reason not to buy;
- Overcome the real objection;
- Review the features and benefits the vehicle has to offer again.
- Ask for the sale again.

(DELIVERING THE VEHICLE)

Once the deal is sealed make sure you take the time to go over the vehicle with the customer in detail. Show them all of the options, features and benefits again making sure they understand how everything works.

Tell the prospect that you want to be their automobile professional for years to come. Let them know (with their permission) that you intend to stay in touch with them from time to time to make sure their auto needs are always met. This will set the stage for them to buy from you again. It also begins the referral process allowing you the opportunity to ask for referrals when you speak with the prospect.

(TOUR THE DEALERSHIP)

Never let the sold customer leave without giving them a tour of the dealership. Make sure you make the time to introduce them to your service manager, body shop manager and even you parts manager.

You goal is to keep your customer returning to the dealership for service on a regular basis. By them visiting the dealership on a regularly this allows you stay in contact with them which allows you the opportunity to ask for referrals again and again.

(Following-Up After the Sale)

If your dealer does not have an in-house CRM follow-up system you need to develop your system of follow up.

You should contact your customers approximately every 90 days. Sned out a newsletter, seasonal postcard, birthday cards, anniversary cards and any thing else that will keep your name in front of the customer.

At a minimum, you should contact your customer every six months.

Building a customer base and maintaining a long term relationship with your customers is vital to your success. If you expect prior customers to buy from you because they did so in the past you are fooling yourself. If you do not stay in touch with your customers believe me you will

become just someone they bought from before. Chances are the majority of your customers won't even remember your name after 3 months unless you do follow up calls and send out letters to them on a regular basis.

(Increasing Write-Up Ratios)

The more people you write-up the more people you will deliver. Attaining higher test-drive and write-up ratios will allow you to reach your sales goal.

LET'S REVIEW
80% of ups that visit a dealership usually buy within 7 to 10 days.
Most salespeople will only write-up about 1/3rd of the people that visit a dealership.
Of 60 ups each month 20 ups are written-up and 40 ups are not.
About ½ of most write-ups are sold.
So, if an individual salesperson sold 10 cars, he probably had 60 ups.
Of the 40 ups not written-up, 20 probably bought elsewhere.

So now do you see the importance of focusing on the 20 ups not written-up? If you do, and you set your goal to write up 70% of your ups you might sell 10 more cars each month.

One of the biggest reasons we don't write more ups is because most prospects will low-ball the salesperson while out on the lot. They will always low-ball you when it comes to what they want to spend and what they expect of a monthly payment.

You must remember that your write-up ratios will remain low if you buy-in to the prospects story.

Another reason we don't achieve a higher write up ratio is because we over qualify the prospect on the lot. We hurry to find out if they have had credit problems in the past. If so, we blow them off as quickly as possible.

Have you ever heard of a co-signer? Most credit-challenged people will find someone with decent credit to co-sign if they want a car bad enough. That takes us right back to building rapport, selling yourself as the salesperson, selling the dealership and then selling them on a vehicle while getting them excited every step of the way. If you make the mistake of asking a prospect on the lot if they can find a co-signer before following the process you have just wasted your time. But don't worry some professional salesperson on some other lot will follow the process and get the sale after the prospect leaves your dealership.

(Increasing Test-drive Ratios)

Increase your test drive ratios and you will sell more cars, period. There is only one way to show the difference of a new car over the prospect's old car and it's called the test-drive.

The test-drive engages the prospects sense of sight, feel, sound, and smell. When a prospect drives a new car the looks, the feel, the sounds, and even smell excites their senses. When this happens it only comes down to getting financed and the money issue.

(REASONS YOUR PROSPECTS DO NOT TEST-DRIVE)

1.We ask the prospect to go for a demo ride. Prospects will usually try to find a way out because again, test-driving is an act of commitment.

2. Again, we don't write the customer up because we think we are wasting our time. Quit asking about the prospect's credit, their planned down payment or anything else while out on the lot. Follow the steps to the sale and try to write every prospect you up. If you do, watch your sales double.

4. The customer fears making a mistake and gets cold feet. You can prevent this most of the time by never asking the prospect to buy before they test-drive.

5. The vehicle they look at is not in drivable condition because it has a dead battery, flat tire, keys missing, or out of gas. If you have an appointment to show a certain vehicle test-drive it yourself before the customer arrives.

**Write up everyone. Set your goals for
70% write-ups and 70% demos and when
you are reaching these goals set them for
80%.**

(Close More Internet Deals)

**Internet leads should be treated like you
would any other up. These customers have
taken the time to sit down at a computer,
research your dealership's inventory and
then email a request for information to
you. They certainly didn't do all that out of
boredom. They are looking for an
automobile. Give them the information
they want, and always offer alternatives.**

Here is an Example:

**You have an Internet shopper who wants a
price on a new Chevrolet Impala. Make
sure you give them the price and all
features and benefits that vehicle offers.
Now go the extra mile. In the same email
make sure you give the Internet shopper**

**the price of any late model Impalas in
stock. Give them a monthly payment**

(Depending on their credit score) with $0 down and always include photos of each vehicle you offer them. Photos sell cars.

If you fall into the trap of assuming that all Internet shopper are only shopping you for the lowest price you are wrong. Most of the time they are shopping price but you will be surprised at how many prospects will see more value in the options and alternatives you offer.

The top Internet sales people sell cars online consistently using emails as their primary means of communication. If you insist on a phone number before communicating with an Internet customer you will lose a tremendous amount of sales each month.

Again, always treat an Internet shopper like they were a lot up. Always answer their questions and send them all information they want. Then send them another email telling them about you and your dealership. Tell them what sets you and your dealership apart from your competitors and why they should buy from you.

Always check for new internet leads every 2 to 4 hours whenever possible. Try to answer every lead and answer every question as soon as possible. Make sure you have some sort of database of all customers so you can keep sending emails and calling the unsold Internet prospect.

Always answer every lead as an individual one. Never use canned emails. Always give the Internet shopper your best price and complete information on every vehicle they inquire about.

Never fail to send a requested price quote. If your dealership refuses to send price quotes they are losing sale after sale every month.

For the most part most online car shoppers want to be contacted by email in the early stages of shopping so make sure you respect that. If you require or insist on a phone number immediately this will cost you a lot of sales.

(NEVER CHERRY PICK LEADS)

If you cherry pick and try to guess which Internet lead will result in a sale you are costing yourself and your dealership thousands of dollars in revenue each year.

The average Internet shopper will travel up to 150 to 200 miles for the right vehicle at the right price so don't hesitate to follow up on leads out of your area. I have sold cars to people 3,000 miles from my dealership by using effective emails? Show the customer the value and give them a reason and they will come.

If a prospect emails you about a certain vehicle they saw online that means the prospect is very serious about buying that vehicle.

If the vehicle the prospect inquired about has already been sold email them and tell them, but offer alternative vehicles. Make sure you send photos and details on each of the alternative vehicles you mention.

(Using Templates vs. Canned responses)

Create multiple templates for follow up. Personalize each one depending on the situation.

Send at least 7 more follow up messages. Most buyers do not answer your first response. This doesn't mean they won't buy from you. Use the BUY or DIE rule. Keep contacting the prospect until they either call or email and ask you to stop. You don't have to pester them, but be consistent.

If you do have the vehicle the prospect inquired about make sure you give them complete information and the price. Send them actual photos of the vehicle. Ask them to call you and schedule an appointment to come and test-drive that vehicle.

Using an UP CARD

If your dealership does not require the use of up cards then I suggest you photocopy this one and use it on every prospect you talk to. If your dealership has a CRM complete the up card, enter the information into your CRM then keep the up card for your personal files. If you use the up cards and keep them you will be able to do follow up for years to come.

CUSTOMER INFORMATION CARD

SALES PERSON_____

CUSTOMER NAME_____

DATE _____ADDRESS _____

CITY _____ STATE_____

HOME PHONE # _____WORK# _____

CELL # _____

EMAIL

ADDRESS:_____

SOURCE (check box) Phone Up _____ Lot Up ___

Internet ___ Referral ___ Repeat ___ Service ___

DESIRED VEHICLE INFO:

YEAR_____ MAKE _____

MODEL_____

COMMENTS: _____

PHONE SCRIPTS

The next few pages are samples of Phone Scripts that work. These are compliments of Todd Hudak and have been added to this book with his permission. The ones for unsold customers have been proven to be highly effective in getting the prospect to keep their appointment, which will result in more sales for you and your dealership.

Some of the phone scripts are for following up with your sold customers. When it comes to most people they object to using phone scripts but I challenge you to re-type and use these for one month and watch your appointments show and your sales rise.

INCOMING PHONE CALL SCRIPT

Good Morning/Afternoon, It's a GREAT Day at 123 MOTORS. This is_____ speaking.

Are you calling about our big sale? It's been crazy around here.

Customer response: _____

I'm glad you called! So I can help you get all the information you want and need . . .May I ask you a few questions?

Are you interested in NEW or USED? _____

What equipment would you like?
Cars   Options Desired:
__ 2 Door   __ 4 door

Trucks _____Reg Cab __ X-Cab__
Cloth__ Leather ____ 2 Wheel_ 4 Wheel__
5 Speed __ Automatic _____
Repeat back to confirm...

If there was a similar vehicle with similar equipment, that was Less expensive, would you want me to let you know about it?
_____YES   _____NO

Are you _____Adding? Or ___Replacing a vehicle?

What are you Currently driving?
Year_____ Make _____ Model _____
Miles _____
Equipment_____

So I can better understand what is important to you, thinking about your current vehicle, What do you Like Best? _____
Will you be trading it in? ___YES ___NO

(IF YES: "In order to get you the most money, we need to see it as soon as possible")
Before we schedule a time for you to come in, Let me check on availability of the_____
from our inventory. This won't take long.
What is your Home# _____
Work#_____ Cell #_____
How do you spell your last name? _____
First name? _____
As matter of fact, to save you some time, let me check to see if that vehicle is available right now? Is that Okay with you?
IF YES: Please Hold(PAUSE)... (Look up how many of the model are in stock) Availability looks good! But we need to act if this is

something you want to take care of in the next few days... or, did you want to put this off for a few weeks?

When is the best time for you to come in?
Today or Tomorrow
Give name, number Morning Evening
and directions   6:15   6:45

Great! We will see you on:_____ @
_____AM or PM
We would like to send you *a confirmation* (NO APPT=*information*) by email...What email address should we use?_____

By the way, have you ever been to 123 MOTORS before?
Have you worked with a salesperson? Do you remember their name? If not, No problem!

If anything changes on our end, I will call you to let you know. If something should change on your end, and for any reason you are going to be early or late, would you please call or email me to let me know?
Customer Name _____
Phone (h) _____ W)_____
Email
address:_____
CALLING THE INTERNET CUSTOMER

Hello, this is _____ with the Internet Department here at 123 MOTORS. May I speak with _____? Hi, _____. The reason I am calling is to discuss your request for information so we can give you all the information you want. I will only need a few moments of your time. May we proceed? (Ok) Have you ever bought a vehicle online before?

Yes - Great! Tell me, how did it go?

No - Let me tell you how our Internet department helps you find the perfect vehicle . . .

There are three easy steps:

1. Find the exact vehicle

2. Give the information you need to make an informed decision

3. Schedule a convenient time to complete the paperwork

You indicated that you are interested in a _____ (list model and equipment).

What other equipment would be important to you? (summarize and explore needs)

Adding or replacing? What are you currently driving? Would you like an estimate?

Year____ Make_____ Model _____

Miles _____Equipment_____

So we can understand what is important to you . . .

Best _____ Improve _____Give
name, number Morning   Evening
and directions   6:15   6:45

Great, we will see you on _____ at _____.
By the way, have you been to our dealership before? Did you work with a salesperson? Do you remember their name? If not, no problem!

Also, do me a favor . . . if anything changes on your end, please let me know and if anything changes on my end I will return the courtesy. Would you like us to update you on new products and promotions as they become available? Best Number
_____ So we don't interrupt you, when is the . . .
2nd Number _____ Best
Time_____Preferred method of contact?
__Phone   __eMail   __Either
When would you like to get your vehicle?
__Days   __Weeks   __Months
Customer Name_____Phone (h) _____
(w)_____ Address _____
eMail _____ Sales Consultant ___
Date_____ Time_____

(CALLING BACK THE NO SHOW UNSOLD PROSPECT)

Hello. This is _____ from _____ 123 MOTORS. May I speak with _____. Am I interrupting anything?

The reason I am calling is because I may have missed you last night and I wanted to make sure that you were treated properly when you visited us.

Has anything changed?

Would it be more convenient for you if we bring the _____ to your home Or place of business?

So we can make it easy and convenient for you to see the vehicle, when would be the best time to meet? Today   or Tomorrow Give name, number Morning Evening and directions   6:15   6:45 Great, we will see you on _____ at _____.

By the way, so we can save you time, I'll have a few_____ (vehicles) pre-selected base on exactly what you have told me.

Also, do me a favor . . . if for any reason you are going to be early or late, please let me know and if anything changes on my end I will return the courtesy.

Would you like us to update you on new products and promotions as they become available?
Best Number _____ So we don't interrupt you, when is the . . . 2nd Number _____ Best Time _____
Preferred method of contact?   __Phone __eMail   __Either

When would you like to get your vehicle?
     __Days __Weeks   __Months
Customer Name _____
Phone (h) _____ (w) _____
Address _____
eMail _____

(NO APPOINTMENT OUT GOING CALL)
(The Be Back)

Hello. This is _____ from _____. May I speak

with_____. Am I interrupting
anything? Are you still looking for a vehicle?

The reason I am calling is to review what you
wanted so we can keep a look out for it.

You were looking for a _____
(year, make, model). Does that sound right?
Is there anything else? What most important
in your next vehicle?

If there was a similar vehicle, with similar
equipment, that was less expensive, would
you consider it?

So that we can find you the right vehicle at
the right time, is this something you want to
do in the next few day, weeks, or months?

So we can make it easy and convenient for
you to see the vehicle, when would be the
best time to meet?
Today   or Tomorrow
Give name, number Morning Evening
and Directions   6:15   6:45
Great! We will see you on . . . By the way, so
we can save you time, I'll have a few_____
(vehicles) pre-selected base on exactly what
you have told me.

Also, do me a favor . . . if for any reason you are going to be early or late, please let me know and if anything changes on my end I will return the courtesy.

Would you like us to update you on new products and promotions as they become available?
Best Number _____ So we don't interrupt you, when is the . . .
2nd Number _____ Best Time _____

Preferred method of contact?   __Phone   __eMail __Either
When would you like to get your vehicle?
    __Days __Weeks   __Months

Customer Name _____
Phone (h)_____ (w) _____
Address _____
eMail _____
Sales Consultant _____
Date_____ Time_____

(CALLING BACK THE SOLD CUSTOMER)

Hello. is _____ there?

This is _____ from 123 MOTORS.

Is this a good time? Am I interrupting anything?

The purpose of my call is to thank you for the purchase of your new _____, and to make sure your experience with us went smoothly.

Do you have any questions or concerns? On a scale of 1 - 10, how do you rate your experience? What would make it a 10?

As you may know, you will be receiving a survey in the mail . . . and if you don't mind, please let me know if anything has occurred that would prevent us from receiving a perfect score.

Would you like to be updated on service and sales promotions?

So you don't miss out on any service coupons or sales promotions . . . let us update our records.
Current Address: _____

Current Phone#'s:_____

**Email Address:_____Number of
Household drivers?_____**

**Would you recommend _____ to
your friends and family?**

(Ask for referrals if it feels right)

**Again, the reason I called you was to thank
you and let you know _____ may
contact you regarding your experience with
our dealership, and if for whatever reason.**

(CALLING PROSPECTS ON MANUFACTURER'S CALL LIST)

**Hello. This is _____ from 123
MOTORS.
May I speak with_____. .. Am I
interrupting anything?**

**The reason I am calling is because _____
Motor Company has asked us to contact you.
Their records indicate you still own a
_____. According to _____**

Motors records, you are currently in a great position to take a look at a new _____.

So we can make it easy and convenient for you to see the _____, when would be the best time to for you to come in? **Great, we will see you on**
_____ **at** _____
We would like to send you a confirmation by email...
What email address would you like me to use?_____.

By the way, so we can save you time, We'll have a few _____ (vehicles) pre-selected .

Also, do me a favor . . . if for any reason you are going to be early or late, please let me know, and if anything changes on my end I will return the courtesy.

We Would like to keep you updated on new products and promotions as they become Available...
What Email Address would you like us to use?_____
Best Number _____ So we don't interrupt you, when is the best time to call?
2nd Number_____ Best Time _____

Preferred method of contact? __Phone __eMail __Either
When would you like to get your vehicle?
__Days __Weeks __Months

Customer Name _____

Phone (h) _____ (w) _____
Email Address_____

Address, City, State,
Zip:_____

Sales Consultant _____

(EMAIL AND LETTER TEMPLATES)

The next few pages are some of the best Email and Letter templates that I have ever used. They are a compilation of some of the best-tested follow up tools ever developed. These are compliments of Todd Hudak, of Hudak Consulting and have been added to this book with his permission. Feel free to re-type and use these. For more information on phone scripts, email templates or follow up letters that work contact Todd Hudak by

visiting his website @
www.Hudakconsulting.com

1 Day Letter Thanks for Internet Request

Date Today
First Name Last Name
Street
City, State Postal Code

Dear First Name,
Everyone at 123 Motors would like to thank you
for inquiring about 123 Motors through the
internet. We appreciate the time and interest you
have shown in attempting to do business with us.
Working together I'm sure we will find a way to
select the perfect vehicle to meet your needs. If you

have any questions or concerns please feel free to call me at anytime.

Sincerely,
Salesperson 1
Sales Consultant
Dealership Toll Free

1 Day Letter Thanks for Purchasing

Date Today

First Name Last Name
Street
City, State Postal Code

Dear First Name,

Congratulations and Thank You for purchasing your Vehicle Year Vehicle Make Vehicle Model from us at 123 Motors. I hope you are completely satisfied with both your vehicle and our dealership.

Please let me know if I can be of further assistance
to you, or if you have any questions or concerns.

Sincerely,
Sales Consultant

1 Day Letter Thanks for Visiting
Date Today
First Name Last Name
Street
City, State Postal Code

Dear First Name,

Everyone at 123 Motors would like to thank you
for visiting our dealership. We appreciate the time
and interest you have shown in attempting to do
business with us. Working together I'm sure we
will find a way to select the perfect vehicle to meet
your needs.

If you have any questions or concerns please feel free to call me at anytime.

Sincerely,

Sales Consultant
Dealership Phone

1 Day Sold Thank You Letter

Date Today
First Name Last Name
Street
City, State Postal Code

Dear First Name,

I want to personally thank you for the purchase of your vehicle from 123 Motors. It is our philosophy to please and service every customer who purchases a vehicle from us. We will all do our part to serve you. We will continue to keep in

touch with you, to listen to your thoughts, opinions, and most of all your suggestions. We want you to be COMPLETELY SATISFIED with every aspect of your experience with 123 Motors. Again, my personal thanks for becoming a part of our valued clientele!
Sincerely,

Sales Manager

30 Day Sold Follow Up Letter - File
Date Today
First Name Last Name
Street
City, State Postal Code

Dear First Name,

It's hard to believe that you have had your vehicle for one month already. Time sure does fly. I hope everything with your purchase at 123 Motors is to your satisfaction. Since you are a valued customer, I thought you'd like to know there is a special program for customers who send their family and friends in to see me. Of course I will work hard to make your referrals feel at home. I can assure you that any person you send to me will be treated in the same professional manner you have experienced. We trust that your new vehicle is performing well, but if anything needs attention, please call or stop by our Service Department. We value you as our customer.

Sincerely,

Salesperson 1
Sales Consultant
Dealership Phone

6 Month Prior to Term End - File

Date Today
First Name Last Name
Street
City, State Postal Code

Dear First Name,

Although there are still several months remaining on your Vehicle Year Vehicle Model lease, it's about time to begin thinking about your next vehicle. The manufacturer continues to provide exciting innovations to its lineup. The most recent models are impressive.

I would be delighted to answer any questions you may have concerning our leasing programs or any of the manufacturer's new models. Please don't hesitate to call!

Sincerely,
Salesperson
Dealership Phone

(no response) - Email

Dear First Name,

I wanted to follow up with you since we have not spoken for a few days. I know that when looking for a new car, the information search can be a very lengthy and involved process. However, hopefully your efforts are beginning to form a solid basis on which to make a final and educated decision. If there are any questions or concerns that you may have or if I can be of any assistance at all throughout your information search, please do not hesitate to contact me at (Dealership Phone Number) or email me at (Salesperson's Email Address). Thank you for your interest. I look forward to hearing from you soon.

Sales Consultant
123 Motors

Internet 1st Response - Email

Hi First Name,

My name is (Salesperson's Name), I am the Internet Consultant for 123 Motors. I have received your request for a Vehicle Model . We do have several Vehicle Model's in inventory. What I would like to do now is speak to you in a little more detail about your vehicle needs. I am sure you know that here at 123 we are the #1 dealer in the area. We offer a great selection of new and used vehicles, and we are experts at establishing or re-establishing credit. I will be trying to contact you by phone, you can reach me directly at (Dealership Phone Number) or feel free to E-mail me at: (salesperson's Email Address).

I look forward to working with you.

Salesperson Name

Second Internet response - Email

Dear First Name,

I have been trying to contact you, but have been unable to reach you. We have access to programs that can save you money, and the inventory to have you driving a New Car Today!

The more I know about your situation the more I can help you. Where exactly are you in the buying process? We work primarily by appointment, so be sure and let me know if you plan on stopping by. You can reach me directly at (DEALER PHONE#) or feel free to E-mail me at: _____.

Again, thank you for your request and I look forward to working with you.

Sincerely,

Salesperson's Name

Trade In Email

Dear First Name,

Thank you for your inquiry concerning the value of your trade. Unfortunately, it is difficult to give you a valid estimate without actually seeing the vehicle, but I would be more than happy to set up an appointment with you so that our professional appraisers can assess the vehicle's condition and estimate an accurate trade-in value. Please contact me at (Dealership's Phone Number) to arrange an appointment. I look forward to working with you to attain a reasonable trade-in value for your vehicle.

Sincerely,
Salesperson
123 Motors
Dealership Phone Number

Final internet response - Email

Dear First Name,

I have made several attempts to contact you by Phone and E-mail, but have had no success. I would love to assist you with the purchase of your next vehicle.

Feel free to contact me directly at Dealership's Phone Number or E-mail me at (Salesperson's email address). I hope that I can be of future assistance to you.

I look forward to working with you.

Thank You,

Salesperson

123 Motors

Dealership Phone Number

Congratulations 1 Year Sold – Letter or Email

Date Today

First Name Last Name
Street
City, State Postal Code

Dear First Name,

Can you believe that it has been 1 year since you purchased your vehicle from 123 Motors? The time has gone by so quickly. I wanted to take a moment to thank you once again for your business. If you have any questions or concerns, or just want to say "HI", feel free to give me a call.

Sincerely,

Sales Consultant
Dealership Phone

Congratulations 2 Year Sold – Email or Letter

Date Today

First Name Last Name
Street
City, State Postal Code

Dear First Name,

Can you believe that it has been 2 years since you purchased your vehicle from 123 Motors? The time has gone by so quickly. I wanted to take a moment to thank you once again for your business.

If you have any questions or concerns, or just want to say "HI", feel free to give me a call.

Sincerely,
Sales Consultant
Dealership Phone Number

3 Year – Congratulations Letter or Email

First Name Last Name
Street
City, State Postal Code

Dear First Name,

Can you believe that it has been 3 years since you purchased your vehicle from 123 Motors? The time has gone by so quickly. I wanted to take a moment to thank you once again for your business.

If you have any questions or concerns, or just want to say "HI", feel free to give me a call.

Sincerely,

Sales Consultant
Dealership Phone Number

Congratulations 4 Year Sold – Email or Letter

Date Today

First Name Last Name
Street
City, State Postal Code

Dear First Name,

Can you believe that it has been 4 years since you purchased your vehicle from 123 Motors? The time has gone by so quickly. I wanted to take a moment to thank you once again for your business.

If you have any questions or concerns, or just want to say "HI", feel free to give me a call.

Sincerely,
Sales Consultant
Dealership Phone Number

Good News Bad News (Orphan Owner) – Email or Letter

123 Motors
Address
City, State Zip Code
513-761-1111

Date Today

First Name Last Name
Street
City, State Postal Code

Dear First Name,
First, I would like to say thanks for the purchase of your Vehicle Year Vehicle Make Vehicle Model. You are an extremely valued customer and as such are extremely important to this dealership and to me. The bad news is that your previous salesperson is no longer with 123 Motors. The good news is that I have volunteered to take over

the responsibility of servicing you and your family with any of your automotive needs. I was not around for the initial sale but I will here for you anytime you need me to help in whatever capacity you request. Here at 123 Motors, we realize that employees sometimes leave us but we never wish to

leave our customers without a representative that they can go to for assistance.

My name is Salesperson 1 and I'm a Sales & Leasing Consultant. Please feel free to call me at (Dealership Toll Free #) if I can be of any help to you, your family, or any of your friends in the future.

I wanted to write this letter to let you know that there is someone here that cares about you and will be glad to help you in any way possible. Please call anytime and just ask for Salesperson 1. If you happen to miss me, please leave a message and I will return your call promptly. I look forward to meeting you in the very near future.

Thanks again!

Sales Consultant
Dealership Phone

Happy Birthday Letter

Date Today

First Name Last Name
Street
City, State Postal Code

Dear First Name,

I just wanted to wish you a very Happy Birthday!

I hope everything is going well and that the year to
come brings you lots of happiness.

Sincerely,

Sales Consultant
Dealership Phone

Happy Birthday Letter – (Another Sample Letter)
Date Today
First Name Last Name
Street
City, State Postal Code

Dear First Name,

I just wanted to wish one of my customers a ....

HAPPY BIRTHDAY!!!

I hope next year brings you all the best!!

Sincerely,
Sales Consultant
Dealership Phone

P.S. Is it time to renew your driver's license?

Author's Notes

If your dealership is in need of sales, Internet, BDC or Management training there is only one person I would call and that is Todd Hudak of Hudak Consulting. You can visit his website at: www.hudakconsulting.com

Todd Hudak is, in my opinon, one of the top automobile sales trainers in the business. I had the pleasure of attending many of his training seminars. Todd Hudak is Mr. Excitement. He knows what and what does not work. If you are a manager or principal/owner of an automobile dealership, and need or want your sales staff highly trained then do yourself a favor and call Todd Hudak by visiting his website.

If you dealership does not have a CRM then I recommend you log onto: www.e-pulsetrak.com And click on THE PRODUCT. This will allow you to see e-pulsetrak.com in action and give you some quick examples of how it can help every car dealer and salesperson in the business. Todd Hudak also sets up and trains dealerships on the use of E-pulsetrak, in my opinion, one of the best CRM's in the business.

About The Author

Douglas Hensley has been in the automotive sales business for over 10 years. He started out as a salesperson and knew there was more to car sales than just meeting and greeting a customer on the lot or answering a sales call. He got busy learning what and what does not work. He worked his way up from a sales person to Internet Director over 5 stores for a dealership group. By using the email templates included in this book he doubled internet sales for the dealership where he was employed. From there he became a GM and then opened, developed and managed a Business Development Department for a Dealership Group. At this writing Mr. Hensley is the GM for a Car Dealership where he trains his sales staff on a daily basis.

www.ingramcontent.com/pod-product-compliance
Lightning Source LLC
Chambersburg PA
CBHW030411290526
45785CB00004B/1968